COOL

SPRINGY, SLINKY & STRETCHY PROJECTS

CRAFTING CREATIVE TOYS & AMAZING GAMES

REBECCA
FELIX

Summit Free Public Library

Checkerboard Library

An Imprint of Abdo Publishing
abdopublishing.com

ABDOPUBLISHING.COM

Published by Abdo Publishing, a division of ABDO, PO Box 398166, Minneapolis, Minnesota 55439. Copyright © 2016 by Abdo Consulting Group, Inc. International copyrights reserved in all countries. No part of this book may be reproduced in any form without written permission from the publisher. Checkerboard Library™ is a trademark and logo of Abdo Publishing.

Printed in the United States of America, North Mankato, Minnesota

102015
012016

THIS BOOK CONTAINS RECYCLED MATERIALS

Content Developer: Nancy Tuminelly
Design and Production: Mighty Media, Inc.
Editor: Paige Polinsky
Photo Credits: iStockphoto, Mighty Media, Inc., Shutterstock

The following manufacturers/names appearing in this book are trademarks:
Aleene's® Tacky Glue®, Craft Smart®, Gedney®, Slinky®

Library of Congress Cataloging-in-Publication Data
Felix, Rebecca, 1984- author.
  Cool springy, slinky & stretchy projects : crafting creative toys & amazing games / by Rebecca Felix.
     pages cm. -- (Cool toys & games)
  Includes index.
  ISBN 978-1-68078-050-5
1. Handicraft--Juvenile literature. 2. Toys--Juvenile literature. I. Title. II. Title: Cool springy, slinky and stretchy projects.
  TT160.F457 2016
  745.5--dc23
                        2015033035

CONTENTS

BOUNCE AND STRETCH!

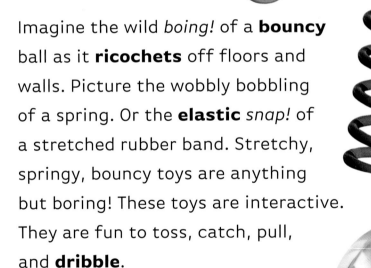

Imagine the wild *boing!* of a **bouncy** ball as it **ricochets** off floors and walls. Picture the wobbly bobbling of a spring. Or the **elastic** *snap!* of a stretched rubber band. Stretchy, springy, bouncy toys are anything but boring! These toys are interactive. They are fun to toss, catch, pull, and **dribble**.

4

ANCIENT BOUNCY BALL

The first rubber ball was used by **Mesoamericans** to play a game in the 1600s.

PRESENT-DAY
USA

MESOAMERICA

CARIBBEAN SEA

PACIFIC OCEAN

Many of these toys have not changed much from their original designs or materials. Each **bounce**, stretch, and springing *pop!* creates big fun!

MAKING RUBBERY, WIRY, STRETCHY TOYS

Toy makers around the world are busy every day making **bouncy** balls, Slinkys, yo-yos, and more. Have you ever wondered how these toys are made? Their materials and shape are key. Many toys that bounce and stretch begin with substances found in nature. **Petroleum**, natural gas, and certain tropical plants are used to make rubber.

A RUBBER TREE

6

Factory workers pour rubber into molds to create **bouncy** balls. Rubber bands begin as long rubber tubes. Springy toys are also made in factories. The Slinky is probably the most famous springy toy. It is a metal or plastic coil that moves in waves and flips down sets of stairs. Slinkys are formed in a top-secret machine that has been used for more than 70 years.

HUGE RUBBER-BAND BALL!

The world's largest rubber-band ball is more than 6 feet (1.8 m) tall and 9,000 pounds (4,000 kg)! It sits in Lauderhill, Florida. Joe Waul created the ball over six years.

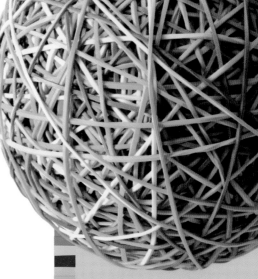

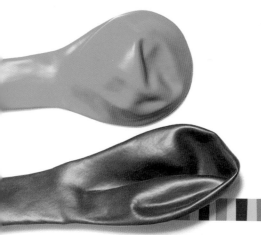

BECOME A TOY MAKER

THINK LIKE A TOY MAKER

Toy makers come up with new colors, designs, and ideas every day. They create rubber dolls that can stretch to twice their size. They make **bouncy** balls that hold tiny figurines and jump ropes that light up. Some modern Slinkys even glow in the dark!

As you create the stretchy, bouncy toys in this book, read the project steps. Look at the photos. Then think like a toy maker! Do the photos inspire you to add any fun twists to the projects?

8

HAVE FUN!

Playing with
bouncy, stretchy toys is fun.
Making them should be too! In this book, you
will build a bouncy ball from a squishy water
balloon. You'll turn a bag of rubber bands into
a stretchy jump rope too.

As you create these bouncy, springy toys,
get creative! Do you want to weave a ribbon
into your jump rope? Did you find a better way
to make the springy yo-yo bounce? Go for it!

MATERIALS

HERE ARE SOME OF THE MATERIALS YOU'LL NEED
FOR THE PROJECTS IN THIS BOOK.

acrylic paint

balloons

cat toy springs

chenille stems

craft sticks

duct tape

foam ball

glove

googly eyes

marker

newspaper

origami paper

paintbrush

plastic Slinky Jr.

pushpins

rubber bands

ruler

scissors

small bouncy balls

stapler & staples

tacky glue

thick rubber bands

WATER-BALLOON BOUNCY BALL

CREATE A BOUNCY BALL BY WRAPPING A WATER BALLOON IN RUBBERY LAYERS!

1 Have an adult help you fill a balloon with water. Fill the balloon until it takes shape and expands a bit.

2 Pinch the balloon as close to the body as possible. Tie the balloon tail in a knot near the body. The balloon should be a stretched, round shape.

3 Trim the extra tail length on the filled balloon.

4 Cut the tail ends of several empty balloons.

5 Stretch a tailless balloon around the filled one. Repeat with several more tailless balloons. The more you add, the **bouncier** the ball will become!

MATERIALS
10–15 balloons
water
scissors

SLINKY

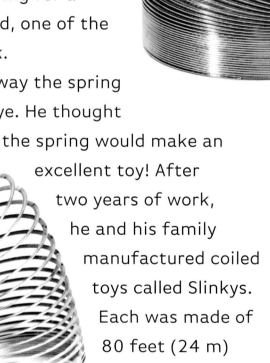

Have you ever played with a Slinky? This popular coiled toy was invented in the 1940s by accident! Engineer Richard James was creating a spring for a marine ship. As he worked, one of the springs fell from his desk.

Something about the way the spring moved caught James's eye. He thought the spring would make an excellent toy! After two years of work, he and his family manufactured coiled toys called Slinkys. Each was made of 80 feet (24 m) of wire.

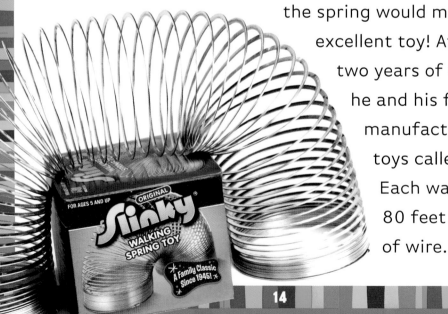

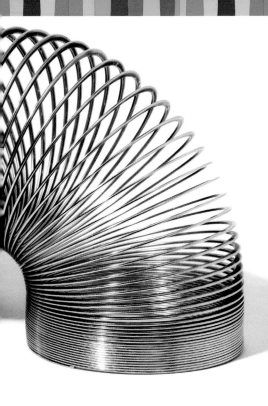

The James family opened a Slinky factory in Pennsylvania. Hundreds of thousands of Slinkys have been created there in the past 70 years.

SLINKYS AROUND THE WORLD

There have been more than 250 million Slinkys sold since the 1940s. If all those Slinkys were stretched out, they would circle the planet more than 120 times!

SPRINGY SPIDER PUPPET

USE SPRINGS AND THINGS TO CREATE A BRIGHT, BOUNCY SPIDER!

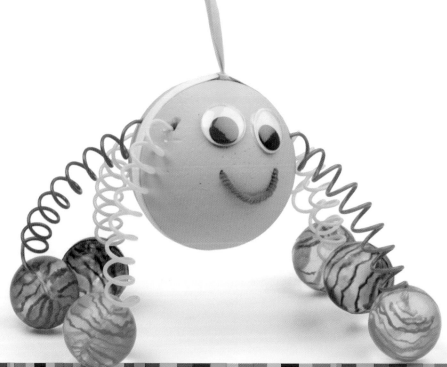

PREPPING THE PIECES

1 Cover your work surface with newspaper. Paint the craft sticks and foam ball fun colors. Let dry.

2 Decide how many legs will fit on your spider. Select a **bouncy** ball for each leg. Carefully poke a hole in each ball with the pushpin.

3 Slowly screw a cat toy spring into each hole. Twist the springs into the bouncy balls as deep as you can.

4 Lightly pull on the spring to make sure its hold is secure.

(continued on next page)

MATERIALS	paintbrush	rubber bands
newspaper	pushpin	tacky glue
2 craft sticks	small bouncy balls	googly eyes
foam ball	cat toy springs	ruler
acrylic paint		chenille stem
		scissors

ASSEMBLING

1 Wrap a rubber band around the foam ball's **circumference**.

2 Loop another rubber band through the first one.

3 Use the pushpin to poke holes where the spider's legs will be.

4 Screw each leg into the pushpin holes on the foam ball.

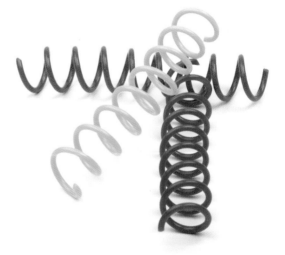

5 Glue on googly eyes. Cut the chenille stem about 2 inches (5 cm) long. Give your spider a smile by poking the ends of the chenille stem into the foam ball.

6 Loop an additional rubber band around the rubber-band loop you made in step 2. Add more rubber bands to make a chain. Wrap the end of the chain around the craft sticks. Wrap them so the sticks make an *X*.

7 Now make the spider jiggle and walk on its springy, **bouncy** legs!

JUMBO PAPER SLINKY

FOLD AND WEAVE PAPER INTO A GIANT WORKING SLINKY!

FOLDING

1 Draw a small *X* at the bottom of a piece of origami paper. Keep the *X* at the bottom through step 8.

2 Fold the paper in half **horizontally**. Unfold.

3 Fold the bottom edge to the center crease. Unfold.

4 Fold the top edge to the crease made in step 3. Unfold.

5 Fold the paper in half vertically. Unfold.

(continued on next page)

MATERIALS
marker
origami paper
stapler & staples

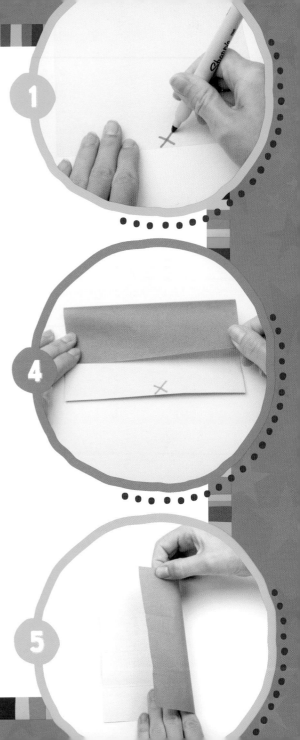

6 Fold both sides into the new center vertical crease.

7 Fold in half again so the paper looks like a tall, narrow book.

8 Lay the piece of paper so the opening is to the left.

9 Fold the bottom up and to the right. Line up the piece's top edge with the upper **horizontal** crease.

10 Unfold the entire piece of paper. Flip it over. The creases should make what looks like an arrow. Rotate so the arrow points to the right.

11 Pinch the crease on the right side. Place your left finger inside the point of the arrow. Push and pinch to fold the arrow inward.

12 Press on all folds to keep the newly made *L* shape together.

13 Repeat steps 1 through 12 to make 30 to 40 pieces.

CONNECTING

1 Take up two completed *L* shapes. Hold as shown.

2 Slightly unfold the ends of the top edges of both pieces. Looking from the side, the end of the shape on the left should look like an *M*. The shape on the right should be an upside-down *V*.

(continued on next page)

3 Tuck one pocket of the V around the far edge of the M.

4 Unwrap the V slightly to wrap it around the M.

5 Gently slide the two pieces together. This may take some adjusting.

6 Repeat steps 1 through 5 to make four-sided squares that connect in a coil.

7 On each end, staple the last two coils together. This will keep the ends from separating.

8 Test your giant Slinky down some stairs, off a box, or in your hands!

RUBBER-BAND JUMP ROPE

LOOP RUBBER BANDS TO CREATE A STRETCHY, COLORFUL JUMP ROPE!

1 Gather four craft sticks and one thick rubber band. Place half the length of the rubber band between the sticks. There should be two sticks on either side.

2 Use a rubber band to secure the sticks.

3 Wrap the craft sticks in duct tape. Add extra layers of tape to create cushion.

4 Loop a rubber band through the open loop of the thick rubber band.

5 Loop another rubber band through the two loops of the first rubber band. Repeat with more rubber bands until your chain is about twice your height.

6 Once your chain is long enough, loop the second thick rubber band through the ends of the last rubber band. Then loop the thick rubber band through itself and pull to create a knot.

7 Sandwich the thick rubber band between the last four craft sticks.

8 Use a rubber band to secure the sticks. Wrap the sticks in duct tape.

9 Have fun using your stretchy jump rope!

SLINKY YO-YO

BUILD A RUBBER-BAND BALL AND ATTACH IT TO A SLINKY TO CREATE A BOUNCING YO-YO!

1. Wrap the **bouncy** ball in rubber bands until it is completely covered.

2. Tuck a new rubber band through a rubber band on the top layer.

3. Loop the rubber band through itself. Then pull to make a knot.

4. Tuck and knot another three rubber bands to the ball. Space them evenly around the **circumference** of the ball.

5. Knot the four rubber bands around two coils of the Slinky at one end.

(continued on next page)

MATERIALS

small bouncy ball
15–30 rubber bands
plastic Slinky Jr.
glove (gardening glove
  or cotton winter glove)

6 Pull on the ball to make sure all knots are secure.

7 Put on the glove. Gather a few coils of the Slinky at the end opposite the ball.

8 Secure the coils to your gloved hand by loosely looping one or two rubber bands around both. Make sure the rubber bands are not too tight or causing discomfort.

9 Gather the coil in your hand and let go. Catch and **dribble** your yo-yo as the ball hits the ground and **bounces** back up!

GLOSSARY

bounce – 1. to spring up or back after hitting something. 2. to throw something down so it hits a surface and springs back up.

circumference – the outer edge of a circle or the length of this edge.

dribble – to bounce something again and again.

elastic – capable of recovering original size and shape after being stretched, twisted, or squeezed.

horizontal – running in the same direction as the ground, or side-to-side.

Mesoamericans – people that lived in a southern area of North America in the pre-Columbian era.

petroleum – a dark-colored liquid that is a fossil fuel. It is used to make fuel, plastics, and other products.

ricochet – to bounce off a hard surface.

WEBSITES

To learn more about Cool Toys & Games, visit **booklinks.abdopublishing.com**. These links are routinely monitored and updated to provide the most current information available.

INDEX